# MOOSE

## OF YELLOWSTONE AND GRAND TETON

PHOTOGRAPHY AND TEXT BY HENRY H. HOLDSWORTH | FOREWORD BY CHARLIE CRAIG

FARCOUNTRY
PRESS

*Above:* "Chocolate moose." Calves are light chocolate brown for their first five or six weeks of life.

*Right:* A cow moose uses her approximately eleven-inch-long ears to scan for signs of danger. Moose can swivel their ears independently in an almost complete circle, and they can detect sounds up to two miles away.

*Cover:* A cow moose and calf wade in the shallows of the Snake River at Oxbow Bend on a beautiful fall morning.

*Back cover:* A bull in his prime rests in a bed of narrow goldenrod.

*Title page:* A cow moose pauses at Schwabacher's Landing along the Snake River.

# CONTENTS

To my wife, Valerie, for putting up with all my moose mistresses; to my daughter, Avery, who has never known a backyard without a moose; and to my golden retriever, Nellie, the only one who wanted to get up for all those sunrise photo shoots.

ISBN 10: 1-56037-492-6
ISBN 13: 978-1-56037-492-3

© 2009 by Farcountry Press
Photography © 2009 by Henry H. Holdsworth

For more information about our books, write Farcountry Press, P.O. Box 5630, Helena, MT 59604; call (800) 821-3874; or visit www.farcountrypress.com.

Created, produced, and designed in the United States.
Printed in China.

14  13  12  11  10  09   1  2  3  4  5  6

# FOREWORD | BY CHARLIE CRAIGHEAD

What is it about a moose that appeals to so many people? They're gangly, homely, often mangy, but people love them. They're ill tempered and dangerous, but visitors to my hometown of Moose, Wyoming, will walk within a few feet of a cow and calf to snap a picture. I've seen tourists pile out of their car just to stand for a photograph in front of the Moose Post Office sign when they can't find the real thing. Even tourists who travel from the far side of the planet to see Yellowstone National Park's thermal pools or the abrupt rise of the Teton Range in Grand Teton National Park will walk away from a bald eagle or a black bear for a chance to see a real moose in the wild.

There's an old photograph, taken in the early 1900s, of a young Jackson Hole homesteader boy and his new pets: twin moose calves. Moose were a surprisingly new part of frontier life back then. Throughout the 1800s there were no moose reported in Jackson Hole by any of the fur trappers or explorers who visited the valley, although they reported the numbers of other species they saw. And in neighboring Yellowstone only a few moose had been sighted by the late 1860s and early 1870s. The summer of 1880 produced half a dozen sightings near Old Faithful, but the population steadily climbed as moose continued to emigrate from northern forests and settle on the Yellowstone Plateau. A U.S. Forest Service census in 1912

Seemingly all legs, a day-old calf high steps its way over obstacles in the morning light.

turned up 47 moose in Jackson Hole. By 1951, an estimated 2,600 moose lived in the state of Wyoming, with about 600 of those living in Jackson Hole. Over the years, moose numbers have fluctuated in Yellowstone and Grand Teton national parks.

Old-timers in Jackson Hole learned to live with moose as four different animals, depending on the season. In the spring they were irritable, wandering bullies to be given a wide berth; in summer they became secretive, defensive animals that disappeared into the willow thickets and river-bottom forests; by late summer and fall those rangy, patchwork animals reappeared as sleek, beautiful, and somehow graceful creatures; and in winter an uneasy truce was drawn when the moose found themselves almost domesticated animals as they were forced by deep snow into folks' yards and onto plowed roads.

I grew up around moose, but in a different way. My parents used to get humorous Christmas cards from old-timers who posed for photos while hanging to the upper limbs of a thin sapling as a moose threatened from below, and I loved the subtleties of the joke. For a local, it was a funny, familiar situation. My mother, who had a wonderful sense of humor, introduced me to the world of moose practical jokes. She took me out in the sage flats one spring to gather dried moose droppings left from the winter months when moose had survived on bitterbrush and willow tips. If I broke open one of the hard, oblong pellets, I'd find nothing but the half-digested sawdust remains of a moose's winter diet. The pellets made a sweet, wild smoke if I lit one and let it smolder as incense. But my mother wasn't after incense—she showed me how to pour melted chocolate over a tray full of moose droppings to make joke candy to hand out to unsuspecting summer visitors. One time, when my brother was in the Peace Corps in Fiji, my mother put together a care package to send him. Things were still rattling around in the box after she'd packed all the items, so she sent me out to gather up a few handfuls of dry moose droppings. This was before the days of foam peanuts, and she filled the voids in the package with the dried-up droppings. We heard later that the package sat in the Fiji customs office for weeks while they tried to determine what kind of drugs were being smuggled in. Eventually my brother got the package, but the suspicious customs officials kept the moose turds.

A road sign near Moran shows the mileage south through the valley of Jackson Hole.

So, I was driving on the Moose–Wilson road recently when I saw Henry Holdsworth's VW van going the other way. I flagged him down and we parked at a turnout to visit. We were both looking for moose; Henry was working on a new book on the animals, and I needed some stock video. We shared notes and compared our recent sightings, and I quickly realized that Henry knew just about every moose in the valley personally. Among others, there was a beautiful, big bull at the Oxbow Bend that liked to hide in the willows as soon as a photographer showed up, a tourist-conditioned cow and her large calf in the old sawmill ponds, and a nervous young bull in the sagebrush near the north end of Blacktail Butte. Henry knew them all. He had lived with a moose in his viewfinder for the past year, through all seasons and all kinds of weather, gathering images for this book. His favorites were the classic, large-antlered bulls that gathered in the sagebrush flats to eat bitterbrush in early winter, and the long-legged June calves at their mothers' sides.

As Henry drove off, I thought about the kinds of images he was gathering and about the old photos of moose taken in Jackson Hole in the 1920s and 1930s. Despite protection, Yellowstone and Grand Teton national parks are different than they were 100 years ago. With climate change affecting the greater Yellowstone area, it seems possible that photographers have witnessed both ends of the moose era in Jackson Hole, and maybe in the higher Yellowstone country as well. I sincerely hope not, but if a warm and dry climate eventually pushes moose back to the cooler northern forests they came from, at least we'll have the spirit of their century-long visit beautifully documented by Henry Holdsworth.

CHARLIE CRAIGHEAD, *from Moose, Wyoming, is a writer and filmmaker who grew up in a family of biologists. He has worked for National Geographic, Wolfgang Bayer, and the Discovery Channel and has written books on a variety of subjects, including a guidebook series for Grand Teton National Park and a book on the historic Wort Hotel in Jackson, Wyoming, titled* Meet Me at the Wort.

*Above, left:* Having just left its den after a long winter's nap, this grizzly would like nothing better than to dine on a winter-killed moose. The bear hasn't eaten since late November or early December.

*Above, center:* Late-April winds ruffle the winter coat of this young bull, which shows the buds of new antler growth.

*Above, right:* Spring comes late to northwestern Wyoming's high country. This June 12 storm dumped eighteen inches of snow in upper elevations.

*Facing page:* A black-billed magpie takes a walk on the wild side as it searches for a meal of winter ticks or other tasty parasites that might reside in this moose's thick coat. This isn't a one-sided relationship; the magpie gets a meal, and the moose gets rid of organisms that could make it sick. If infested with ticks, a single moose could accumulate as many as 50,000 of them over the course of one winter.

# SPRING

Spring comes slowly to the mountains and valleys of Yellowstone and Grand Teton national parks. Not until April does winter begin to loosen its icy grip on the land. By May, melting snow has given way to new growth, in the form of bright-green grasses and budding trees. In June, wildflowers once again grace the landscape, and the rebirth of the land is nearly complete. The high country is ready for a new generation of moose to enter this wild and beautiful world.

In preparation for this new life, cow moose separate themselves from their yearling calves and find a secluded place to give birth. The calving period takes place in late May or early June, with most calves born during a single two-week period. The synchronized timing of the births creates a smaller window of vulnerability for the mothers and their newborns, and it comes at a time when new plant growth provides cover and good quality food for nursing females.

While cows with newborns keep to themselves in spring, bulls often form bachelor groups of two to four individuals. Together they follow ancient routes to summer feeding grounds, consuming as many calories as possible to nourish their growing antlers and add bulk for the fall mating season. Their antlers covered in "velvet," bulls take great care not to damage them until growth is complete in late August. In fall, the powerful bulls with their great racks will become the center of attention in the moose world—but for now, the gangly, milk-chocolate-colored calves steal the show.

*Above, left:* Roughly two weeks before giving birth, a cow moose chases off last year's calf. The cow will often become very aggressive to encourage the yearling to set out on its own.

*Above, right:* Less than twenty-four hours old, a newborn rests, hidden in the willows. Calves typically weigh between twenty-two and thirty-five pounds at birth.

*Facing page:* Following a gestation period of about 231 days (almost 8 months), a pregnant cow moose seeks a secluded spot to give birth. This takes place in late May or early June, which allows her calf as much time as possible to grow and become strong before winter. She will alter her birthing site from year to year to avoid patterns that might attract predators.

*These pages:* The word "moose" is derived from an Algonquin word loosely meaning "eater of twigs" or "he who strips bark off young trees." During a spring snowstorm a cow moose *(facing page)* shares a creekbed with a kingfisher *(above, left)* and a nesting sandhill crane *(above, right)*. Birds such as sandhill cranes and red-winged blackbirds sometimes confront or dive bomb moose if they get too close to their nesting sites.

*Right:* A mother moose keeps a watchful eye while bedding down in the tall grass. Unlike elk and other members of the deer family—which hide their calves and leave the area to feed, returning later to nurse their young—moose keep their babies close at all times. Should a predator such as a grizzly, black bear, wolf, or coyote attack, cow moose use their sharp hooves to aggressively defend their young.

*Below:* In early June a grizzly bear searches for elk and moose calves in the willows along Yellowstone's Indian Creek, in the area known as Willow Park.

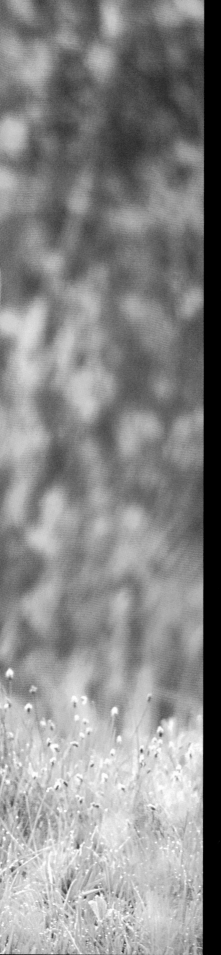

*These pages:* A day-old calf
nose to the ground for b
it struggles to its feet. M
stand within hours of bi
begin walking not long a
particular calf became b
left eye during birth, lik
by a stick or other sharp

*Right:* A cow moose dines on aquatic plants. During spring and summer, moose may eat three to four times as much as they do during the winter, when the animals survive on less-nutritious twigs and bark.

*Below:* A two-week-old calf takes a break from nursing. In its first few months, a moose calf drinks about half a gallon of milk every day, which allows it to gain as much as four pounds in twenty-four hours. By mid-September, when the calf is weaned, it will weigh between 250 and 300 pounds.

*These pages:* The summer sun rises over Yellowstone Lake *(below)* while a cow moose dines along its shoreline *(facing page)* and a great blue heron looks on *(left)*. Moose are found across most of northern Europe, Asia, and North America. From the time its ancestors migrated across the Bering Land Bridge from Siberia to present-day Alaska some 75,000 years ago, the moose has evolved into four distinct subspecies across the northern United States and Canada. The Shiras moose is the smallest of these, and it inhabits the Northern Rocky Mountains, including Yellowstone and Grand Teton national parks.

*These pages:* A two-month-old calf samples a diet of new leaves and aquatic vegetation. At this age the calf is eating mostly solid foods, learning from its mother what plants to eat as the summer progresses.

*Above:* A two-day-old calf tests its new legs. By the time it is five or six weeks old, it will be able to outrun a bear; but it will stick very close to mom just in case.

*Facing page:* In a case of life imitating art, a cow moose pauses next to a pair of great blue heron sculptures in a Jackson lawn. She found the pond a good place to drink and the birds just right for scratching an itch.

*These pages:* A cow moose *(above)* stands her ground and stares down a coyote looking to make a meal of her calf. There were a pair of coyotes working together, but, knowing they were outmatched, they did not show serious interest in pursuing the cow and her calf. The coyotes moved along in search of easier prey, and mother and baby *(right)* take one last look to make sure.

*Facing page:* An expecting female takes cover in some thick willows. Given its size, it's amazing how quickly and quietly a moose can disappear.

*Below:* A grizzly with three yearling cubs in tow combs the thickets of Willow Flats in Grand Teton National Park. With four hungry mouths to feed, she will scour the area like a bloodhound in search of elk and moose calves from late May into early July.

*Right:* A cow and her calf find food and cover in a Jackson neighborhood not far from the Snake River. With a growing population of grizzlies and wolves in the Greater Yellowstone Ecosystem, some cows have learned to stick close to areas of human development to avoid predators.

*Below:* Twin calves line up for mom at Bridge Bay near Yellowstone Lake. Where moose populations are growing, sightings of twins are frequent. In areas overpopulated by moose, twins are rarely seen.

*Above, left and center:* A homemade sign in downtown Wilson and a moose-crossing sign near Moran Junction signal that it's time to slow down in places moose frequent.

*Above, right:* A cow moose wades into a wetland to feed on aquatic plants.

*Facing page:* After creating its first "moose jam," this calf learns that summer brings a deluge of visitors to Yellowstone and Grand Teton national parks each year.

# SUMMER

In moose country, summer is a time of plenty. Moose indulge themselves in the bounty of plant life, often foraging for up to ten hours a day, consuming forty to sixty pounds of vegetation every twenty-four hours.

They are never far from water, dining almost constantly on aquatic plants that grow in area rivers, lakes, and wetlands. Abundant and nutritious foods help moose add weight after the lean winter months, as well as feed the growth of bulls' antlers and transform the spindle-legged calves of spring into the confident youngsters of summer.

As snowpack recedes, some moose head to the high country of Yellowstone and Grand Teton national parks in search of better forage and relief from biting insects. Because they easily overheat, moose also seek cool mountain air and shade from intense summer sun. While many cow moose stay in the same area for much of the year, bulls may travel up to twenty miles between seasons.

Moose also make themselves at home in the water, where their excellent swimming skills and long legs serve them well when feeding on water lilies, exploring islands, and crossing rivers swollen with summer snowmelt. Watching a moose disappear underwater only to emerge with a mouthful of plants is a true north-country treat. Summer is indeed a wonderful time to enjoy the splendor of moose country.

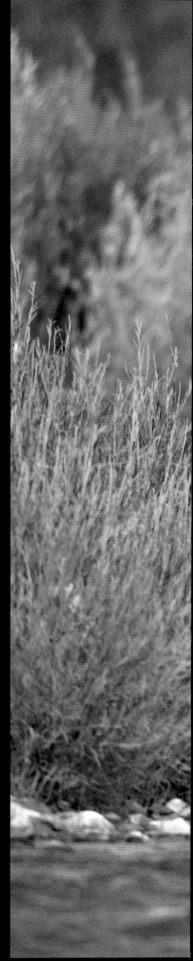

*Right, top:* A shy cow takes a peek through a chokecherry bush.

*Right, center:* A two-month-old calf shows the first hint of a dewlap, or bell, under its chin while shedding what's left of its light-colored baby fur. Both males and females develop dewlaps.

*Right, bottom:* A cow dines on aquatic plants in the mirrorlike water.

*Far right:* Moose antlers are broad and palmate, unlike those of other members of the deer family. Size, symmetry, and growth rates are determined by an animal's age and health, as well as the quality of available food. Antler size increases as a bull ages, peaking around eleven to thirteen years of age; antler size decreases after that. Moose in the wild can live fifteen to eighteen years or more under ideal circumstances; the oldest moose in captivity lived to the age of twenty-two.

*Above, top and bottom:* The partially blind calf *(above, top)* I found on its birthday in spring checks me out some three months later. Its left eye appears to have healed, and the calf is still going strong. I stayed with this calf like a babysitter while mom *(above, bottom)* fed in the pond.

*Left:* An afternoon shower does not deter this cow from a late lunch.

*Facing page:* This bull enjoys the bounty of late summer in the high country, far up Cascade Canyon in Grand Teton National Park. Cooler temperatures, fewer insects, and high-quality food, such as this mountain ash, are reasons for many moose to migrate vertically as the summer progresses.

*Below, left and right:* Moose don't hesitate to hit the trail and head for higher elevations in the summer. Remember to keep your eyes open when traveling in the backcountry. You never know who might be just around the corner.

*These pages:* This cow moose has learned to cool off, snack, and take a "bubble bath"—all at the same time.

*Above:* A calf always has its mother's ear *(top left)*, and surprisingly calves do quite a bit of vocalizing. Just a little scratch *(top right)* hits the spot. Ears aren't only for listening *(bottom left)*; they also keep summer pests somewhat at bay. Although this calf *(bottom right)* is getting big, it is never far from mom.

*Facing page:* By late August this calf has grown large enough to spend more time out in the open, but mother and young are rarely more than fifty yards apart.

*Above:* Along the Lewis River in southern Yellowstone National Park, a bull moose is cloaked in mist. This bull sports a fine-looking dewlap, perhaps the most unusual feature of a moose's anatomy. Variations in dewlap size and shape help moose identify each other, especially in winter, when antlers have been shed. Biologists use them to distinguish individual animals as well, and some believe dewlaps may serve as a cooling device—although their full purpose remains a mystery.

*Left:* An early-morning fog is brought on by cooler temperatures as summer winds down in late August.

*Above:* Cows may not give birth every year. When this cow did not produce a calf in the spring, her twins from the previous year, one male and one female, stayed with her throughout the summer. She still treated them with tenderness, and, although the male calf spent more time with other young bulls after the rutting season, the female stayed with mom right through the ensuing winter.

*Facing page:* A cow and her male yearling share a late-summer snack of willows.

*Facing page:* A young bull in velvet pauses in a wetland after munching on a lunch of cattails. Moose have a varied diet and are known to eat several hundred different types of plants in North America and some twenty-five to thirty species in any one area. They know just what plants to eat at different times of the year for optimal nutrition.

*Below, left and right:* A cow moose snacks on aspen leaves and exchanges glances with a great gray owl.

*Above:* A bull moose emerges from a stand of young lodgepole pine trees. The 1988 Yellowstone fires not only changed the landscape of the park, they altered the dynamics of its moose population. Loss of winter habitat in old-growth lodgepole pine, known to contain healthy populations of subalpine fir trees, a key winter food source for moose, may be leading to a decline in moose populations within the park. Other factors that can affect moose populations throughout the Greater Yellowstone Ecosystem are winter range overgrazing, an increase in predators such as bears and wolves, human activities, drought, and climate change.

*Right:* This cow moose has all her ducks (or, in this case, pelicans) in a row—but she still does not want to share her sandbar.

*Above:* Two young bulls take a dip in the Snake River. Moose are excellent swimmers and have been known to travel as far as ten miles in the water.

*Left:* A cow and calf drink at the shore of Jackson Lake as the sun sets behind Mount Moran.

*Right:* After shedding his velvet on September 9, a bull crosses the Gros Ventre River, leaving Grand Teton National Park for the National Elk Refuge. The far bank provides cottonwood trees and shade on a sunny day. Moose can overheat in temperatures above 57 degrees Fahrenheit, which is why you rarely see them at midday in summer. The best time to look for moose is at dawn and dusk, when temperatures are cooler.

*Below:* As summer comes to an end and antler growth ceases, bulls begin to shed their velvet, revealing the hard bone beneath. Shedding usually occurs in the first two weeks of September, with peak activity between the fifth and the tenth. Once the shedding has begun, the bull will do its best to get rid of the velvet in one or two days.

*These pages:* After growing their antlers for three to four months, a change in testosterone levels signals these bulls to shed their velvet and get ready for "the rut," or mating season. No longer worried about damaging the tender velvet, bulls almost immediately try the new racks on for size and begin the process of determining dominance over rivals *(below, left)*. Once a bull has shed his velvet, his disposition changes, and the gentle giant of summer becomes ornery and unpredictable. At this time of year, it is especially important to keep a safe distance.

*Right, top to bottom:* With most of the velvet cleaned off their antlers, bulls begin polishing them on trees and small shrubs. This helps remove any dried blood and shines them up to a nice white or light brown.

*Far right:* Bulls dine on grass beneath the Teton Range at Oxbow Bend. They have been eating forty to sixty pounds of plants per day over the course of the summer in order to be in their prime when the rut begins in early September. For the next three to six weeks, they may eat little or nothing at all while searching for and attracting potential mates.

*These pages:* Along Christian Creek, in Grand Teton National Park, a cow moose watches as her frisky calf prances about on a frosty September morning. After romping around for a while and kickboxing with a hapless pine tree *(above)*, the calf determines it's time for a little nap *(facing page)*.

# FALL

Fall is a magical time in Yellowstone and Grand Teton national parks. The first snows of September add a sugar coating to the high peaks, and aspens bring a golden glow to the valleys. Soon, the sound of bugling elk fills the meadows. There is a sense of excitement in the air that is unlike any other time of year—the feeling that something remarkable is about to begin. It's rutting season, when bulls battle each other to prove their dominance and win the right to mate and pass on their genes.

"The rut" begins in early September with the shedding of velvet, resulting in newly exposed, blood-red antlers contrasting with the bright yellows of willow leaves. Bulls surge with testosterone, transforming from the gentle giants of summer to the hot-blooded Casanovas of autumn.

When heavy morning frost and snow in the high country cue them to head for lower ground, bulls are on the move, using their amazing senses of smell and hearing to locate potential mates. If two rivals of equal size should fancy the same female, a mighty, and sometimes deadly, battle ensues. These clashes are rarely seen, and the outcome can be swift, but to witness these powerful animals at war is truly remarkable. To the victor go the spoils, and the genes of the toughest bull carry on in the next generation.

*Above:* As the autumn colors emerge, bulls search for prospective mates in traditional breeding areas—and sometimes attract a crowd. The chance to see moose, bears, wolves, and other wildlife amid incredibly beautiful scenery draws visitors from around the world to Yellowstone and Grand Teton national parks.

*Right:* The first rays of sunrise greet a majestic bull moose as he crosses the Snake River at Oxbow Bend in Grand Teton National Park.

*Above:* Aspen leaves, buds, twigs, and bark are year-round staples for moose.

*Left:* A cow and her four-month-old calf get a bath and a hearty breakfast beneath glowing cottonwood trees.

*These pages:* A one-year-old tries his luck and his strength against a seasoned bull *(above)*.
The old master was quite gentle with his understudy; when he had finally had enough,
one mighty shove with his antlers sent his young rival away, dejected *(facing page)*.

*These pages:* Making tracks, a young bull hoofs it down from the high country through Phelps Lake on the Lawrence S. Rockefeller Preserve in Grand Teton National Park.

*Above:* A five-month-old calf takes in the rituals of the rut through a vignette of autumn color.

*Right:* A cow leads her calf away from a persistent bull, which stands in the trees behind them, just outside the image. With plenty of willows, aspen, and water, the Oxbow Bend of the Snake River is one of the best and most scenic places to see a moose in the entire Greater Yellowstone Ecosystem.

*Left:* A bull in his prime makes a river crossing.

*Facing page:* In the throws of a lip-curl, this bull has found a ready mate.

*Below:* Willow Flats, along Jackson Lake in Grand Teton National Park, is paradise for moose. With water and willows stretching for miles, Willow Flats supports one of the densest moose populations in the Greater Yellowstone Ecosystem.

*These pages:* A bull uses all his senses to locate ready mates. After listening intently and following a female's scent, he approaches cautiously. He then performs a lip-curl (known as a Flehmen response), which exposes a special organ in the nose, allowing him to detect her readiness to breed. If she is ready, he will rest his head on her back and see if she resists his advances.

*These pages:* A bull *(above, top left)* keeps a watchful eye on a prime female *(above, top right)*. If she is not ready to mate, she may try to run away from him, and he will give chase *(above, bottom left and right)*. The cow decides when, where, and with which bull she will breed. Once breeding has taken place, the bull will move on *(facing page)*; dominant bulls can mate with as many as ten to twenty females during the rutting season.

*Above:* After being bluff charged by a rutting bull elk, a brave moose calf pushes
his luck, knowing that mom will back him up if he gets into trouble. A second charge
by the elk brings mom to his defense, and both learn that a set of antlers trumps
size in this match-up between members of the deer family.

*Facing page:* Young elk and moose check each other out on a frosty morning along
a river bottom.

*Right, top:* Young bulls watch the older males and imitate their rutting behavior. Even one- and two-year-olds sometimes battle it out to show who will be the dominant bull in years to come.

*Right, center:* Three's a crowd in this showdown of future kings.

*Right, bottom:* An outmatched yearling takes his frustrations out on a picnic table.

*Far right:* Youngsters imitate the lip-curls of the older males. Bulls do most of their breeding between the ages of five and ten, when they are at their physical peak.

*facing page:* A young male is left on the sidelines during the rut; the dominant bull has chased him away from a group of females.

*Below:* The rituals of the rut are well underway by the third week of September. A bull digs a wallow, or muddy pit, and urinates in it; then he rolls in the wallow, soaking his underbelly, antlers, and dewlap in a distinctive moose brand of perfume *(top left)*. His pungent smell helps accelerate estrus in potential mates—and entices the cow to roll in the wallow as well *(top right)*. A female calf studies these ancient rites of fall *(bottom left)* and imitates the wallowing behavior *(bottom right)*.

*Right, top:* Moose on the run can reach speeds of thirty-eight miles per hour.

*Right, center:* A tender moment between a cow and young bull.

*Right, bottom:* This bathing black bear poses little threat to an adult moose. Large bears will prey upon newborn calves and bulls injured during the rut.

*Far right:* Now five months old and fully weaned from its mother's milk, a calf munches golden willow leaves. Moose feed on willows year-round, eating different parts depending on the season.

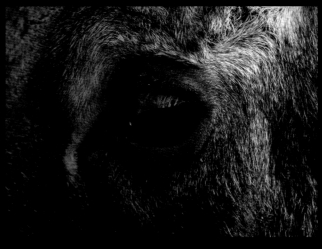

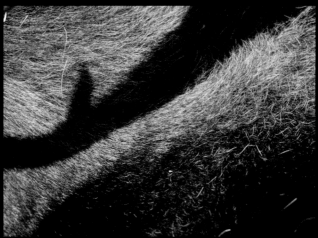

*Above:* Moose have split hooves *(top left)*, which provide sure footing on muddy or spongy ground. They have excellent eyesight *(top right)* and are particularly keen to movement. Moose rest and sleep lying down *(bottom right)*. When resting, a moose will chew its cud, breaking down food to aid digestion by its four-chambered stomach. A dense, wooly undercoat covered with long, hollow guard hairs *(bottom right)* helps keep moose warm during tough Wyoming winters.

*Facing page:* After a long night courting in the light of a full moon, a sleepy bull scratches his back while resting in the shade. One of the most endearing qualities of a moose is its nose. A moose muzzle is more than twenty inches long. Inside are millions of sensory cells; their exceptional sense of smell is 4 times that of most dogs and 200 times better than our own.

*Right, top:* Disease or injury while a moose is in velvet can lead to deformities in antler growth.

*Right, center:* A young bull checks out a pair of courting mule deer, which occupy similar habitat at certain times of the year.

*Right, bottom:* Moose must also learn to share the sagebrush with bison in early winter, giving them a wide berth.

*Far right:* An October sunrise paints the sky in pastels over Blacktail Butte and the Teton Range.

*Above:* Sparring matches can break out anytime after velvet has been shed. Not an actual fight, sparring is practice for when the real battles occur. These harmless altercations take place between bulls that have already established dominance and do not involve the use of full strength.

*Facing page:* Moose are generally quiet animals, but they do occasionally vocalize with each other. Cows and calves use squeals and grunts to communicate. During the rut, females use a series of grunts and groans to indicate their readiness to mate. Bulls, such as the one pictured here, use a low, woofing sound to attract or communicate with females during the rut. On a cold, still morning these vocalizations can carry for miles. Many of the sounds that moose make are at a frequency humans cannot hear.

*Right, top:* When two equally matched bulls walk stiff legged, with their heads swaying in unison, it means a real clash of titans is about to ensue. This particular battle ended when the antlers of one of the bulls snapped, sending him scurrying away.

*Right, center and bottom:* Biologists have fitted radio collars on a number of moose in the Greater Yellowstone Ecosystem to better understand their habits and migration patterns.

*Far right:* A harvest moon over Willow Flats means there will be much activity in moose country tonight.

*Left:* As the rut winds down, bull moose may start to feed again—if they are not distracted. During the height of the rut, bulls may stop eating for up to eighteen days and lose up to 20 percent of their body weight.

*Facing page:* A bull moose exhibiting a Flehmen response is hot on the trail of a female in heat.

*Below:* September snowfall forces moose down from the high country to areas such as the Oxbow Bend in Grand Teton National Park.

*Above:* As the heavy snows of winter set in, moose move to lower elevations, such as river bottoms. This cow and calf just happened to be in my backyard.

*Right:* It can snow any month of the year in the Yellowstone and Grand Teton areas. This bull uses a stand of young aspen trees to hone his antlers in mid-September.

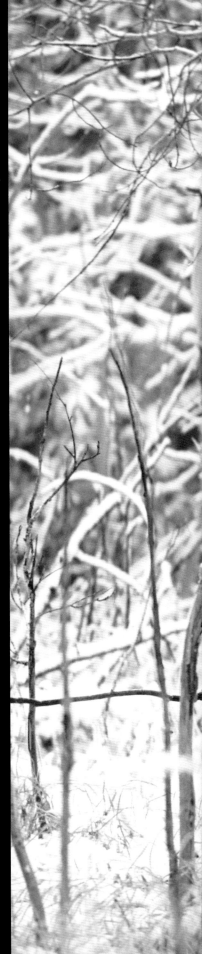

*Above, left:* A bull checks a cow for late-season mating potential.

*Above, center:* With her ears pinned back, her head down, and the hair on her neck and hump standing up, this cow means business. If you see a moose exhibiting this body language, get away quickly. Luckily, in this situation she was aggressively chasing away another female who had eyes for her bull.

*Above, right:* Even during the rut, the safety and comfort of her calf remain this cow's top priority.

*Facing page:* An October snowstorm blankets the valley near aptly named Moose, Wyoming. There is nothing better than a cold snap to keep the intensity of the rut at its peak.

# WINTER

In Wyoming, winter is like an old friend that overstays his welcome—and can show up unexpectedly on virtually any day of the year. Wintry weather may frost the landscape on the Fourth of July, dump two feet of snow in the middle of June, or bring a blizzard on Labor Day. By far the longest season of the year, winter chases autumn away in November and often refuses to retreat until April or May.

The harsh season presents the toughest test to moose and other wildlife in the high country, which can see temperatures of 60 below zero and snow accumulations of five feet or more. Some say that moose are made for winter, with their long legs, thick coats, and taste for willow, aspen, and fir. But as the snow gets deeper and deeper, moose leave the upper elevations and descend to the valleys and river bottoms.

In November and early December, moose often move into sagebrush flats to feast on bitterbrush. They can sometimes be seen in small herds of ten to twenty animals that mingle a bit but don't seem too comfortable with the crowd.

From late December into early January, bulls shed their antlers. With mating season behind them, the antlers are of no use; losing them helps conserve energy as well, which is needed in order to survive times of sparse forage. Their crowning glory cast aside, bulls are now difficult to distinguish from cows, except at close range.

As the relentless snowfall enshrouds their food sources, moose migrate to stands of willow and forests containing fir and aspen. They will do their best to stay hidden from predators such as wolves and conserve their strength.

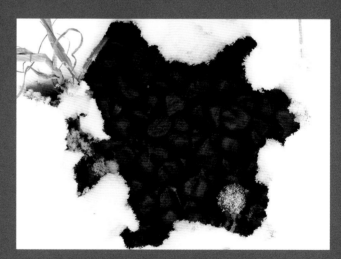

*Above:* Snow blankets a resting bull *(top left)*. Cow and calf hunker down in a blizzard *(top right)*. A six-month-old calf makes its way through the deep snow *(bottom left)*. These are not Hershey's Kisses *(bottom right)*. By examining moose scat, you can tell what a moose has been eating and where it has been.

*Facing page:* As the rut winds down, bulls are less apt to avoid each other.

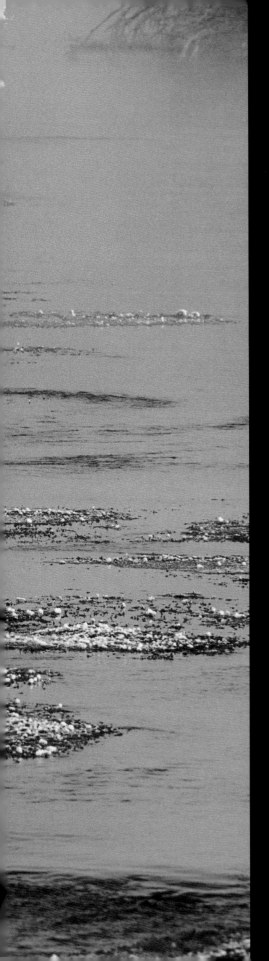

*Above:* A lone wolf might lick its lips at the thought of a meal of moose, but without the teamwork of the pack, it would have no chance of bringing down a healthy adult animal.

*Left:* When the snow gets deep, moose can travel and feed along rivers and creeks. If the water is deep enough, moose can use them as escape routes, evading predators such as wolves, whose legs aren't nearly as long. Wolves are the moose's main winter predator, although mountain lions can take moose in some portions of their winter range.

*Above:* Even into mid-November, two evenly matched bulls may fight if the chance to breed persists *(top left)*. The two titans clash at full speed *(top right)*. By twisting his antlers and driving his opponent backwards, this bull hopes to best his rival *(bottom left)*. To the victor go the spoils *(bottom right)*.

*Facing page:* When the fight comes to an end, the dominant bull may try to gore his opponent, or at least give him a send-off he won't soon forget.

*Above, left:* This young calf was orphaned when its mother was hit by a car. It remained in Wilson, Wyoming, for the rest of the winter.

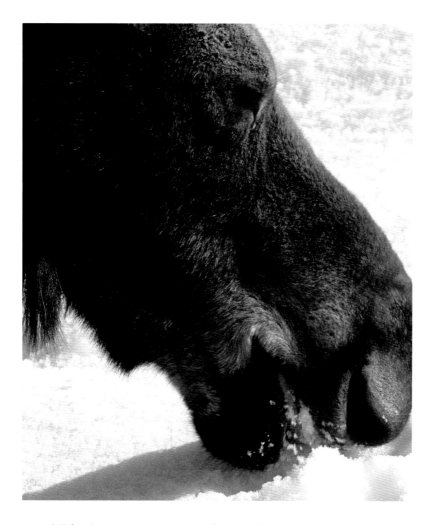

*Above:* With winter temperatures as low as 60 below zero, finding water can be difficult. Moose must often eat snow to stay hydrated.

*Right:* A cow breaks trail for her calf as they make their way through the deep snow. Depending on elevation and location, Yellowstone and Grand Teton national parks can receive 150 to 450 inches of snow in a single winter.

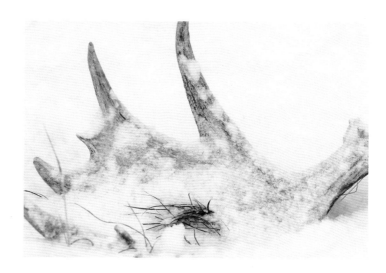

*Left, top to bottom:* With mating seaso antlers are no longer necessary; them between mid-December ar January. The largest bulls with t racks are generally the first to sh smaller bulls following suit soon When the antlers are dropped, b runs from the antler sockets *(top)* quickly heal *(bottom)*. Shed antlers to find *(center)* and cannot be lega from the parks. Birds and rodent mice, voles, and porcupines gna antlers, which are rich in calciun minerals.

*Far left:* A bull with one remaining entices a young rival to assist hir removal. Antlers usually drop wit or days of one another.

*Right:* An aspen grove makes a nice home for a wintering cow moose. It provides shelter from the wind, twigs and bark for food, and cover from predators.

*Below:* A long-tailed weasel would be happy to find a moose antler to chew on while hunting for mice beneath the snow.

*These pages:* Although these two bulls have dropped their antlers, a challenge is still a challenge. Bulls must prove their dominance throughout the year, and without their racks they make lightning-quick strikes with their sharp hooves. A moose's legs are its most deadly weapons, and, if it stands its ground, it can keep most predators at bay.

*Right:* Once bedded down in the snowy sagebrush, a moose can be surprisingly difficult to see.

*Facing page:* In early winter, moose often head for the open country, where they dine on bitterbrush. Although they are solitary for most of their lives, it is not uncommon for moose to gather in small herds of twenty to twenty-five animals this time of year.

*Below:* The reintroduction of wolves to Yellowstone has restored much of the natural balance that was missing for most of the last century. From the original fourteen wolves released in 1995 and an additional seventeen in 1996, there are now more than 200 wolves roaming the Greater Yellowstone Ecosystem. There are ten to fifteen packs in Yellowstone and three packs currently based in the Tetons. Wolves are expected to have minimal impact on moose populations because elk are more plentiful and easier to prey upon.

*Above:* No matter the time of year, if you want to find a moose, just look where the willows grow.

*Left:* When the snow is deep, it's much easier to take the streets. A cow joins her calf on a holiday stroll through a Wilson, Wyoming, neighborhood.

*Following page:* November flurries have this moose looking toward a long winter.